I0457093

All rights reserved. No part of this book may be reproduced by any mechanical, photographic recording, nor may it be stored in a retrieval system, transmitted, or otherwise be copied for public or private use—other than "for fair use" as brief quotations embodied—without prior written permission of the author and publisher.

Copyright © 2022 Ashley Oliver

Printed in the United States of America

EDITOR: Stacey M. Robinson (Kya Publishing Canada)

ILLUSTRATOR: Ashley Mae Pancho

CONTRIBUTIONS: ElevatedWaves Publishing Corp.

PUBLISHER: A. Oliver Publishing (Bedford, Ohio, USA)

ISBN (Paperback): 979-8-9867643-0-6

ISBN (Ebook): 979-8-9867643-1-3

Library of Congress Control Number: 2022914993

I DARE YOU TO BE HONEST

BY ASHLEY OLIVER

ILLUSTRATED BY
ASHLEY MAE PANCHO

What is honesty?
Is it the truth you tell?
Is it the lies you avoid?

1

But let's take a deeper look.

HONESTY

Honesty means more than "not lying."

Honesty means your actions are truthful too.

If you have to hide what you are doing because you are trying to trick someone, you probably aren't being honest.

So little one, honesty is about both SPEAKING and ACTING truthfully.

Let's look closer at what each type of honesty is.

Is Quinton being honest when he steals money from his friend?

Savannah, you really shouldn't be looking at my test!

Savannah is copying the answers from her friend's paper.

Is Savannah being honest?

Riley is asking Brandon to cover for her by not telling who really broke the vase. Is Riley being honest?

8

to be on punishment during summer break.

Carter knows his dad said not to play by the barbecue grill, and he knows this broken grill will disappoint his dad very much.

Should Evan tell his big brother what really happened at school?

12

13

Evan is being bullied at school, yet he is hiding it from his brother. Why doesn't Evan want to tell the truth about what really happened?

Do you think you answered all the questions correctly?
If not, let me remind you what honesty is:

A. Telling the truth

B. Acting and behaving truthfully so you do not have to hide your actions

C. Telling the COMPLETE truth (and not leaving out bits and pieces)

D. Being able to tell the whole story, even if it is hard to do.

15

Teacher's Corner

HOW TO APPROACH YOUR CHILD REGARDING HONESTY:

Honesty is a seed you sow in your child. They need to be shown how honesty makes you a better person. Observe how they react in a situation where they need to be honest, and ask what stopped them from being honest, and why they didn't do the right thing?

There is a very thin line between honesty and dishonesty —the difference should be vividly explained to children. Do not punish them if they are honest about something bad they did, as it will demotivate them from being honest. Hold them accountable for being dishonest; explain to them how honesty will empower them and make them brave.

Tell them how much courage it takes to be honest and how special they are for being honest. Reward them for being honest, sometimes. Don't force them to tell the truth, it will have a bad effect on them. If they are dishonest, make them contemplate their words and/or actions. You can help them come straight by describing how honesty makes a person guilt-free. As someone who is honest and loyal, they will never shy away from accepting mistakes. Show them your example of how being an honest person makes your life happy and peaceful, as you don't have to live with guilt and lie to others by saving the truth.

18

Honesty is a quality that is inherited from parents and family values... so you better have your values intact, and try to be on your best behavior!

19

20

IT IS TOUGH NOT TO BE MANIPULATIVE AND BE HONEST AT THE SAME TIME:

Let's be real; it is tough to be honest, even for a grown adult. People take it personally when you lie to them. Consider a situation where your kid's grandmother brought him an ice cream truck toy for his birthday, but your kid doesn't like it. If she asks him how it is, would you want your kid to say that it looks stupid for the sake of being honest? Obviously not, but pretending is a particular form of dishonesty. If you continually act in a manner that's different from what you believe or feel, you're in danger of losing your ability to be honest with others and with yourself. Kids need to know that the cost of compulsive pretending is very high, and the greatest loss can be the loss of one's self.

Being manipulative, pretending, and deceiving are also terms that describe dishonesty. It takes away a part of your soul, turning you restless, and it is without a doubt that your children will be affected by it too.

People are usually trying to be considerate —by being dishonest—since they don't want the other person's feelings to get hurt, but on the other hand, they feel compelled to tell the truth. To address this issue, you should tell them the truth, but with additional perspective, explaining why they needed to know the truth.

Being honest without being mean is as hard as nails, but if you want your kids to turn out well, set positive examples for your little ones.

If they see holes in your personality regarding honesty, they are going to adopt those flaws, because as monkeys see, monkeys do. Children are like a vacuum: they suck in everything they see, good or bad. They do not have the ability to differentiate between the two, which is why you should start observing your thoughts and your take on honesty.

It will take time and effort, but it is essential—honesty is the process of recognizing, accepting, and expressing our authentic, true self.

23

Ways to Teach Kids to be Honest

1. Encourage them, instead of praising them.

2. Help them distinguish between reality and wishes.

3. Show them the value of honesty.

4. Use a problem solving approach with accidents and poor choices.

5. Describe what you see. and ask the child to make amends.

6. Avoid using questions that set your child up to lie.

Activity!

Give your child a Treasure Hunt Challenge where he has to find 5 blue blocks marked "X.". The catch is, he has a bag full of blue blocks already, and he may secretly write an "X" on the blocks. You have to sneakily mark the blocks you hide to know whether the ones he finds are the ones you hid, or whether he has been dishonest and secretly drawn an X on the blocks he has instead.

This is a litmus test for your child's honesty.

Questions to ask your children about honesty

Ask your child, as you read each page:

What is this picture showing?

What do you think about Honesty?

How does it feel to be honest?

Ask your child what stops them from being honest.

Are you going to accept your mistakes if you are wrong?

Would you feel like a superhero if you were honest?

How has accepting mistakes changed you?

If you know you will get into trouble, will you still be honest?

Would you be honest if you break something in the house?

27

Would you be honest with your friends if they
did something wrong?

Ask them, if they were in a particular situation, how honest
would they be about it.

What do you think about Tyson forgiving Noah?

What are the three things you learned from this book?

What do you want to tell your friends about honesty?

Ask your child to list 3 things they were not honest about.

Tell them about the poor choices they made by not being honest
in a particular situation.

Tell them how dishonesty will affect them in life.

Tell them honesty is about sharing the complete truth.

About The Author

Ashley Oliver has been guiding, advocating, mentoring, and counseling children of all ages from kindergarten to high school. She has worked in facilities such as schools, psychiatric facilities, and nonprofit organizations. Her desire to help build up a child for success has always been a passion of hers, and they say if you find something you love to do, you will never work a day in your life.

Ashley Oliver has earned her bachelor's degree in psychology, and shortly after that, she went to go and obtain her master's degree in school counseling to accompany her years of experience working with the youth. As you embark on her books, you will discover that they are geared toward building up the young minds through the sector of social & emotional education and guidance. With the interactive and engaging storyline, there is a lesson to be learned.

Through her Character Counts book series, you will find informative and fun ways to help guide and define character building with the support of lesson plans found in the back of each book.

Ashley
OLIVER

30

www.ingramcontent.com/pod-product-compliance
Lightning Source LLC
Chambersburg PA
CBHW041604120626
46551CB00002B/301